ISBN 0-7683-2062-3

Text by Flavia and Lisa Weedn
Illustrations by Flavia Weedn
© Weedn Family Trust
www.flavia.com

Published in 1999 by Cedco Publishing Company
100 Pelican Way, San Rafael, California 94901
For a free catalog of other Cedco® products, please write
to the address above, or visit our website: www.cedco.com

Printed in Hong Kong

The artwork for each picture is digitally mastered using acrylic on canvas.

With love and gratitude to those kindred spirits whose dedication, endless support,
and talented hands made this book a reality – Lisa Mansfield, Jane Durand, Diana Musacchio,
Tyler Tomblin, Jennie Sparrow, Solveig Chandler, Hui-Ying Ting-Bornfruend,
Kim Gendreau and Annette Berlin.

Lovingly Dedicated to

From

Date

A JOURNAL OF LOVE

# Blessings of Motherhood

Flavia and Lisa Weedn

Illustrated by Flavia Weedn

Cedco Publishing Company • San Rafael, California

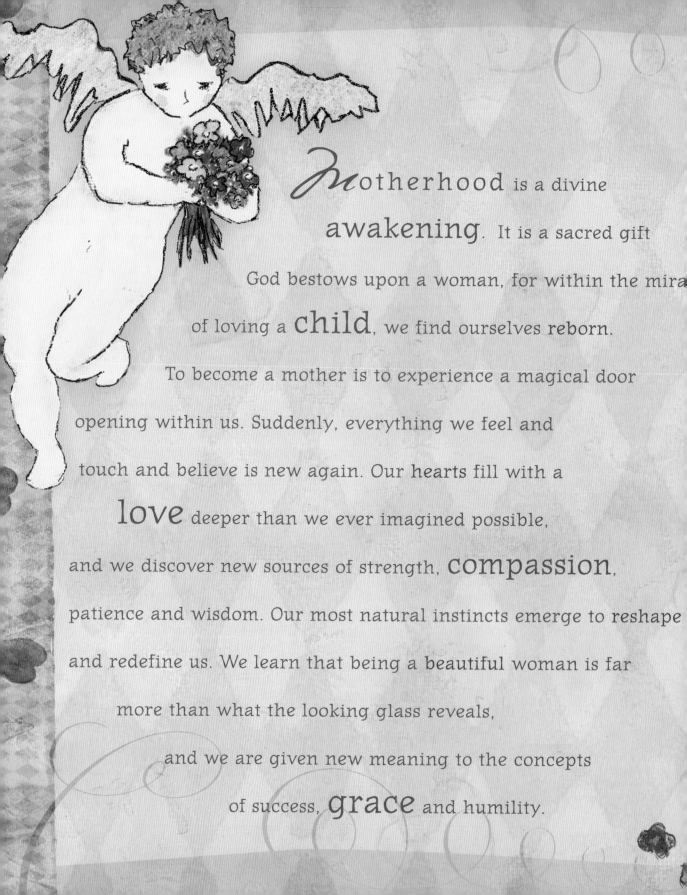

$\mathcal{M}$otherhood is a divine

awakening. It is a sacred gift

God bestows upon a woman, for within the mira

of loving a child, we find ourselves reborn.

To become a mother is to experience a magical door

opening within us. Suddenly, everything we feel and

touch and believe is new again. Our hearts fill with a

love deeper than we ever imagined possible,

and we discover new sources of strength, compassion,

patience and wisdom. Our most natural instincts emerge to reshape

and redefine us. We learn that being a beautiful woman is far

more than what the looking glass reveals,

and we are given new meaning to the concepts

of success, grace and humility.

Motherhood teaches us to let go of lesser surface illusions and to embrace that which really matters — to love and to be loved.

As you journey through all the new stages of this meaningful time in your life, it is important to stay in touch with the woman and the mother you are becoming. As you grow and learn alongside your precious child, may these pages be a quiet companion of support and encouragement; a sanctuary to help you celebrate your soul.

By the time you close these pages, you will have a cherished gift to give your child in years to come. Your personal legacy of love, hope and courage, wrapped in the tale of a shared beginning, will reveal one of life's finest gifts — the heavenly blessing of motherhood.

*Flavia*

# CONTENTS

## Becoming More

## A Mother's Eyes

## A Lifetime's Love

$\mathcal{M}$OTHERHOOD reveals

a part of us we never knew existed.

Like a long-awaited reunion on a path

leading to FOREVER,

we find **peace** with

our place in the world.

It is a place of awe, wonder,

and the beauty of

EVERLASTING love –

a place we were

always meant to be.

# The Dawn of Life

# A Family Is Born

# The Miracle of You

When

a child

comes into

your life, it

fills a special

place inside

your heart – a

place you never

knew was

empty.

# Feeling the Newness

# Of You & Me

# First Whispers

# To My Little One

Into

some

hearts

love brings

a bit of

heaven.

Welcome to

the world,

dear little

one.

# Quiet Contemplation

# Of the Woman in Me

# Private Thoughts

# To Your Father

The

beauty

of the love

we share

makes room

for more. You

are my hero,

and together

we make

dreams

come

true.

# The Wonderment

# Of New Life

 never knew the miracle

it would be to hold you in my arms,

to touch your face, your tiny hands,

or to gaze into the PURITY of your eyes.

I never imagined the sleepless nights,

the SOOTHING beauty of a lullaby,

or the way your presence and the gift of

your love would magically transfor

all of our lives. Bless you, sweet bab

for bringing light into our wor

# Our Changing World

# New Routines

# New Priorities

Embrace
every new
beginning.
Change
brings
wisdom
to the
heart
and
soul.

# Sleepless Nights

# Tender Tears

# Questions I Have

# Fears I Hold Inside

The

deepest

feelings

live in

words

unspoken.

Be unafraid

to share

the voice

of your

heart.

# Challenges We Face

# Strengths Within Me

# Growing Closer

# What Matters Most

Nothing

is more

important

than to

love and

to be loved.

# Seeing with the Heart

# Coming from Love

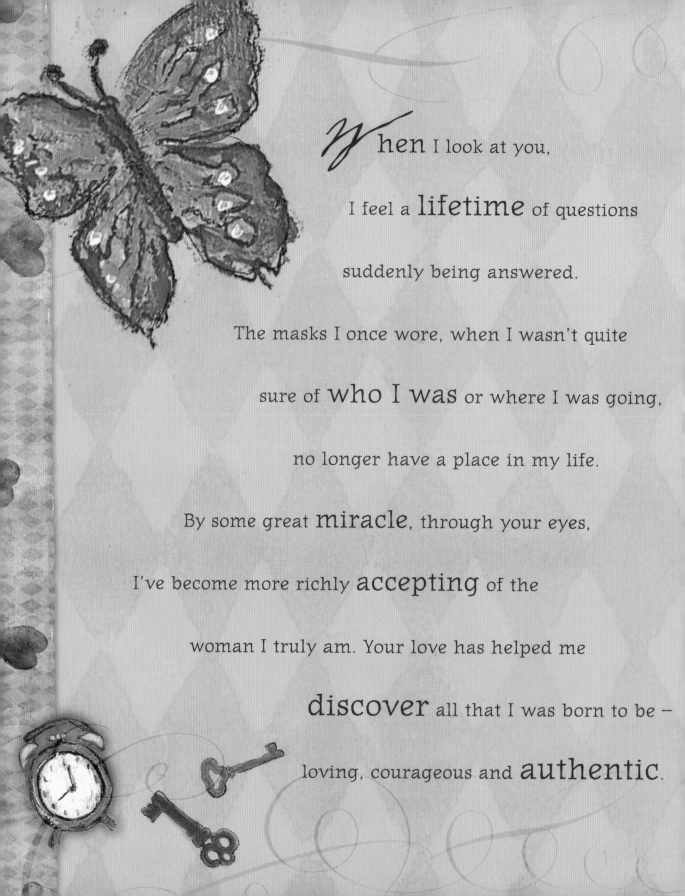

When I look at you,

I feel a **lifetime** of questions

suddenly being answered.

The masks I once wore, when I wasn't quite

sure of **who I was** or where I was going,

no longer have a place in my life.

By some great **miracle**, through your eyes,

I've become more richly **accepting** of the

woman I truly am. Your love has helped me

**discover** all that I was born to be –

loving, courageous and **authentic**.

# Redefining Me

# The Woman I Am

# The Girl I Was

I want

you to

know the

best of me,

the depths

of me,

the tapestry

of my life

and the truth

of my soul.

# The Mother I Am

# The Child in Me

# The Partner I Am

# The Lover in Me

I'm still

the woman

I've always

been, only now

I have new eyes to

see, new love to

give, new thoughts

to bear, new

truths to

share.

# My New Self

# My New Body

# Gifts of Patience

# A New Appreciation

Children

hold the gift

of innocence.

When we open

our eyes to

their wisdom,

we find the

wondrous

simplicity of

life's

beauty.

# The Meaning of Love

# Life & Motherhood

When I think upon my life,

and that which makes up the very

fabric of me, I think of the girl I was and

the woman and mother I've become. I find

wonder in the gift of time, the preciousness

of this sweet life, and the true

miracle of love. I revel in the dreams

you've made come true, and each time you reach for

my hand, my heart knows

that, together,

we're beginning

a new dream.

# Becoming More

# Growing with You

# Learning & Loving

In many

ways

we are

growing up

together.

You are

my finest

teacher

in this

classroom

of life.

# Joys of Nurturing

# Soul Nourishment

# New Levels of Us

# Love and Intimacy

*There are moments when I am so in awe of the person you are, I want to stop time and hold you and the moment forever.*

# Surfacing Reflections

# Of My Own Childhood

# Laughter & Light

# Our Daily Rituals

You bring

love, laughter,

bright light

and sweet magic

into our lives.

How very

blessed are we.

# The Journey Unfolds

# Forever in Awe

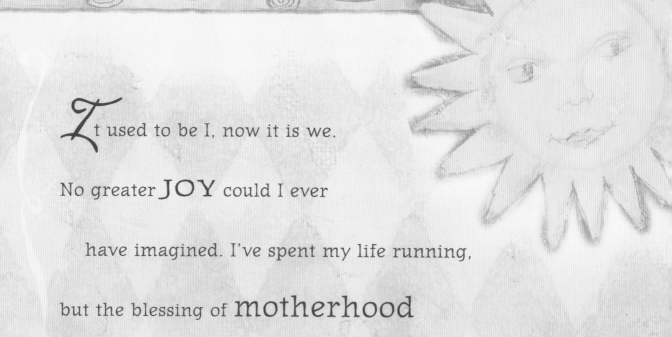

It used to be I, now it is we.

No greater JOY could I ever

have imagined. I've spent my life running,

but the blessing of motherhood

has finally taught me to walk.

Through these new eyes, I shall

strive to help you see the WONDER in every day;

for you, my precious child,

are teaching me the same.

# Home & Family

# Heart & Soul

Love

is the

sanctuary

of the soul.

Wherever

we are,

as long

as we're

together,

we are

home.

# Yesterday's Illusions

# The Beauty of Now

# Defining Success

# What Happiness Is

Life has

a way of

bringing us

refinement

and clarity.

All of my

yesterdays

were only a

prelude to

the splendor

of today.

# Living My Passions

# Finding Time

# The Best of Life

# The Best of Us

You,

my precious

little one,

complete me.

You are the

finest part

of me, and

because of you

I know why

I am here

and where

I belong.

# The Finest Gifts

# The Greatest Teachings

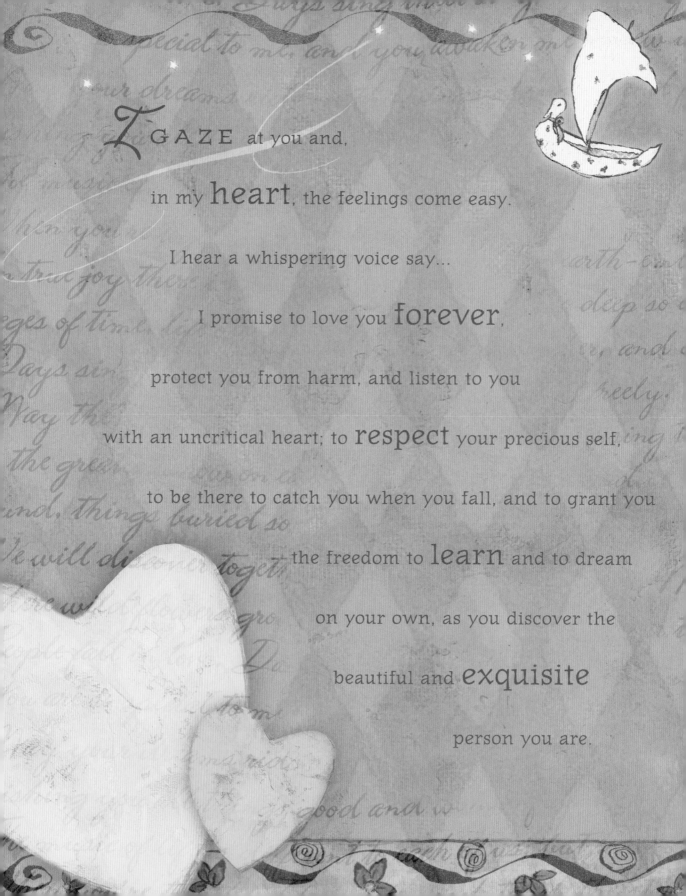

*I* GAZE at you and,

in my **heart**, the feelings come easy.

I hear a whispering voice say...

I promise to love you forever,

protect you from harm, and listen to you

with an uncritical heart; to respect your precious self,

to be there to catch you when you fall, and to grant you

the freedom to learn and to dream

on your own, as you discover the

beautiful and exquisite

person you are.

# A Lifetime's Love

# Peaceful Dreams

# Wishes for You

May

your heart

run free in its

pursuit of

beauty and truth;

may you know

the glory of life

untainted by fear;

and may you

always be

surrounded

by love and

gentle

hearts.

# Prayers of Love

# My Faith and Beliefs

# Traditions I Embrace

# Legacies I Give You

If,
while you
are a child,
just one
someone
loves you
uncritically,
then you
will have
love to give
for the rest
of your
life.

# My Hopes for Us

# Promises I Make

# I'll Always Remember

# Forever in My Heart

I give
to you
a golden
thread of love
and hope and
faith. Its strength
can never be
broken, for it was
made in heaven,
nurtured through
the ages, and
designed
to be yours
forever.

# For You Little One

# A Lifetime of Love

Flavia

Lisa and her daughter Sylvie

Photos by Chris Chandler

Flavia Weedn is one of America's leading contemporary inspirational writers and illustrators. Offering hope for the human spirit, Flavia portrays the basic excitement, simplicity and beauty she sees in the ordinary things of life. Her work has touched the lives of millions for over three decades.

Lisa Weedn, Flavia's daughter and co-author, shares her mother's philosophy and passion. For over fifteen years, Lisa's writings have been a quiet messenger of the fundamental truth that age has no barrier on feelings of the human heart.

Their collaborative work, which celebrates life and embraces meaningful core values, can be found in numerous books, collections of fine stationery goods, giftware, and lifestyle products distributed worldwide.

Flavia and Lisa live in Santa Barbara, California.